There's
Gotta Be
A Little
SUNSHINE
SOMETIMES

There's
Gotta Be
A Little
SUNSHINE
SOMETIMES

Poems, Prayers, Pensées

crista b. griffin

Order this book online at www.trafford.com
or email orders@trafford.com

Most Trafford titles are also available at major online book retailers.

Printed in the United States of America.

ISBN: 978-1-4669-0501-6 (sc)
ISBN: 978-1-4669-0500-9 (e)

Trafford rev. 01/13/2012

 www.trafford.com

North America & international
toll-free: 1 888 232 4444 (USA & Canada)
phone: 250 383 6864 ♦ fax: 812 355 4082

CONTENTS

BUGS

Introduction

Sometimes I sits and thinks and sometimes I just sits—coming to terms with mental illness.

I hear voices. I call them bugs. You don't want to hear them. Definition of bug: 1) creepy crawly thing or maybe a microbe. 2) a disease. 3) a defect or flaw in some system. 4) a listening device. 4) to listen in on. 6) someone who listens in on. 7) an irritation, aggravation, or annoyance. 8)to irritate, aggravate, or annoy.

Bugs seem to have a speaking vocabulary of less than fifty words. They make one, two, or three word analytical or judgmental running commentaries on my life.

I think some bugs are a form of organized crime.

Ever hear about good bacteria that fight off bad bacteria in your body when you are sick? The good bacteria I call wanna-be angels. The only thing angels and bugs have in common is they both listen in on us. Angels, however, are sent from God and are mobilized via prayer. Therefore, they have a right to listen.

Bugs may be demons or fallen angels.

Bugs earn angel wings via putting God first and doing good deeds, e.g. fighting off or extinguishing bad bugs as God wills.

I pray that all bugs be made into love.

Should good names be found
to call creepy-crawlers on the ground?
to make them acceptable to God
and those who turn the sod?
  What about bugs who are disease?
Should I find names that are sure to please?
Such as what? I now do ask.
Am I really up to the task?
  Listening in on is what some bugs do
Or else they're a device so that we can too.
They irritate, aggravate, and annoy
(no matter what definition I could employ?)

3-03

When called: stupid, bad, *!*, or boy
I feel emotionally paralyzed; unable to feel joy.
Over and over I've heard these things said,
and most people say it's all in my head.
  These voices come from outside it seems to me,
and I wonder when, oh when, will they just let me be?
Why do the things they say bother me so much?
It's callousness or mal-intent from each such and such.
  The voices distract me from everyday life
and I think I'd prefer complete absence of strife.
It's hard to make progress in just being me,
when the bug between my eyes won't let me properly see.

8-20-04

What is the proper role of a bug?
Are they even created of God?
Without Him nothing was made that was made?
(until mankind had to turn the sod?)
   Tho it may be true bugs aerate the soil,
Worms signify the soil is good.
Worms aerate and fertilize
better than bugs ever could.
   The early bird catches the worm,
so even birds prefer worms as food.
How do you make a bad thing good?
How do you love your enemies who are rude?

                                                    5-22-08

6

Fat people are more observers
than participants in the arena of life.
Thus Oprah Winfrey stated one time,
tho this opinion might not be rife.
   If the above statement is true,
I should have been observing, not observed,
for the past eighteen years.
Is that absurd?
   Only fat people should be bugs;
the skinny should express their selves—
acting, doing, creating, serving,
whether engineering or dusting shelves.
   Obesity is prevalent in our nation.
I think the desire to just observe prevails.
Doing and accomplishing are expected too much.
Food and drink as a cop-out avails.

                                        6-5-10

Father, God, thank you for loving me.
I apologize for needing reassurance.
Bugs hating me are a trial for sure,
a test of my endurance.
   Please show me how you want me to be,
what to say and what to do,
so that I better love,
and reflect well upon you.

6-6-10

God,

Please forgive me for not being more penitent. Also, please forgive me for feeling superior to bugs tormenting me with analytical, judging, testing comments. Please forgive my anger, hate, and irritability towards bugs, and guide me always to do your will. Please make my anger be righteous, and me be justly tolerant. Please allow me to see any good in bugs.

Where should I be, Lord
Who should be with me?
I cannot see clearly
So just R.S.V.P.
　It seems when I ask of you,
only bugs Your response hear.
How do you expect me
to hold You dear?
　They are always
louder than You.
When I try to be quiet,
they make me blue.
　Why do you allow them
to hear anything?
Do they deserve it?
Happiness do they bring?
　Do they even
try to deserve
Your favor and guidance?
Did I strike a nerve?

　In a classroom
of rowdy, bratty kids
does the teacher speak
as if to the one humble child?
　No.—Does the one humble child
hear what the teacher says?
Or go deaf?

10-17-10

What is the purpose
for bugs to be?
They had to learn what it's like
less than worthless to be?
　It's a job for God's kingdom
to help them out;
and for God's representatives
to know what they're about.
　Yell at some kinds.
Others you squash under your shoe.
Those who are good
are wanna-be angels for you.
　Unobtrusive, even unnoticeable,
or presence of Godliness,
mobilized via prayer
when your life's a mess.
　God directs angels.
Bugs have to earn angel wings,
via learning and loving,
good tidings to bring.

3-27-11

Hard-hearted, slow-minded, stubborn,
are typical bugs' mindsets.
They're not going to listen to me
unless holy spirit lets.
   To most I've been just a *!*
with only tough-love to share.
They prefer one-another
and don't know how to care.
   Remember the flea needs the dog;
the dog doesn't need the flea;
so when you suck blood and provoke,
remember the dog is greater than thee.

   It must be tough to be a parasite
and less than useless be,
to your host on whom you depend
who treats you with animosity;
   scratching at you with claws
and trying to bite you too.
As a parasite,
what then should you do?
   Dream of being better
than you are right now.
Imitate your favorite creature;
love can show you how.

3-31-11

A person who has a broken leg
won't want another with a broken leg,
to help him get around
because they both would have to beg.
  My dysfunction is memory
I can lose my train of thought.
Two heads are better than one,
schizophrenic or not.
  My eyes are weak also;
schizo and nearsighted too.
Eyeglass makes my depth perception poor,
so in more than one way my eyes are blue.
  Who could complement
these sorts of disabilities?
Good eyes and good memories are rare;
Jesus holds the keys
  to regaining my mental health.
I wish the bugs would just shut up.
God, be strong in my weakness.
Jesus, fill my cup.

4-23-11

Who should not be treated as a friend in Christ?
Any who know what they do,
in continually badgering, pricking, persecuting
so God's Spirit in you is made blue?
   If Christ on the cross forgave those who knew not,
shouldn't we presume the same?—
that those persecuting us know not either,
and so are not to blame?
   Nobody knows all consequences
of everything they do or say.
To each has been given a measure of faith;
see that you use yours in the best way,
   that you are able to perceive
(Sometimes you need to trust your gut—
Giving the benefit of the doubt can be like a lie
To yourself and to God is what).
   When you do or say something
that may or may not be wrong
in God's sight, repent quickly
to make life a better song.

4-24-11

14

In what ways are bugs stupid:

They think Satan can win against an all-knowing, all-powerful, God, who is everywhere, and is Truth, Love, Life, Light, Good, Eternity, and Infinity.

4-26-11

From bugs:
  Something beautiful
is one who ages well,
whose face and voice are good,
who keeps us out of hell.
  Jesus must be awesome;
our Father even more;
better than any heros
from earthly folklore.

5-11-11

To bugs:
  Jesus doesn't want you
to cling to one who climbs
up the avalanche of life.
He wants you to find
  your own path out of your vices.
He'll help you in your pains,
if you truly turn from sin
and believe in Him for gains.
  Those who endure until the end
He clothes in righteousness.
Humility and kindness are key
to achieving Godly success.
  Beauty is in the eye of the beholder,
so beauty you have within.
Become more like Jesus;
like him hate all sin.

5-15-11

Father, God, may I have words to say
to reflect upon You in the best way.
May my eyes be not too blue
from focus on bugs instead of You.
  May I learn to converse
as well as write.
May I not be driven
to incite nor fight.
  If I sin may it bring about
greater glory to You,
and a greater good for all
as You want it to.

5-17-11

Jesus, I flew off the handle
because God-damning bugs gave me peace.
Tho not loving as I would want to be loved,
immediately aggravations ceased.
    Please help me to not get perturbed
at minor irritations of life,
and to keep a loving attitude
not cut like a jagged knife.

6-11

God, please make me be
not easily provoked.
And make my attitude good
even where I'm broke,
  so I won't fly off the handle
at hateful, arrogant, bugs,
whose whole life seems to be
wrecking lives like garden slugs.
  Should I drown them all in beer
as good farmers do?
Or would it be better
to just squash them under my shoe?
  The voices of bugs are distant;
they are not available to me
for doing either method
of killing them, you see.
  Please make them be something better
as they serve no good purpose for thee;
I truly need a long, long, vacation
From them to really be free.

7-19-11

Confusion and anger
resulting from hate-crimes
and language mix-ups
and dirt and grime,
   left me feeling
beat and spent;
intolerant of bugs,
I try to repent.
   Instead of being
provoked and annoyed,
I want to love
and be employed—
   if possible leaving
the world a better place
for future generations
of the human race.

7-26-11

When I get grouchy
my voice gets deep,
so bugs call me "boy",
abuse they heap.
   How might I express
my aggravation
in constructive ways
in this free nation?
   (so that I
can win this war
against bug entities
and not be sore
   about them causing
some sex deviation
in myself or others
of God's creation . . .).

9-9-11

   Roaches, ants, and palmetto bugs
think they're heaven sent.
I've got a mind to sue them
for retroactive rent.
   Somehow or another
they think they own my house.
They stubbornly persist here;
I would prefer a mouse.
   Uninvited and unwelcome
bugs know they are here.
We squash them quite often;
I think they thrive on fear.
   My cat, the mighty hunter,
is quick to kill them too.
I refuse to fear bug germs.
I will not sing bug blues.

9-16-11

THOUGHTS ON

POLITICS

Step on the other guy
before he steps on you,
and keep up your defenses
that's the so-called realists' view.

Suck life out of your adversary
to build yourself up,
and thus make him feel
like a hurt little pup,

unable to function
well at all,
emotionally crippled
and not on the ball . . .

Superpower mentality
with or without the U.N.
instead of reaching a consensus
is the war mentality of old Republicans.

8-25-04

Once upon a time
right was said to make might;
meaning God gives you might
if your side is right.
   The U.S.A. gained
much power on this earth;
imposing our systems on other nations, however,
means we need to rethink our worth.
   Once upon a time
crossing our borders was free.
Anyone could come and go
our great nation to see.
   'Give us your huddled masses
yearning to be free'
meant anyone could live and work here
a citizen to be.
   Once upon a time
the U.S.A. believed in free trade,
not taxes on imports
or on goods other countries made.
   Our country thinks it's great
because God is on our side.
Isn't it time we get back on God's side
to be worthy of this great pride?
   'America Loves a Winner'
the Olympics used to say.
So be careful whom you scapegoat,
they could be the winners someday . . .

                                        9-24-05

The battle is the Lord's,
so should warriors blindly follow
their leaders into war
unto death and sorrow?
   Is it theirs
 to not question why?
Instead is it theirs
to do or die?
   Or might they as well
fight wars with words
using bible verses
as sharp, sharp, swords?
   Or is that being
just as bad
as anyone in any war
this world has ever had?
   Good triumphs over evil
and right makes might.
So warriors should sharpen their minds
and walk via faith not sight.
   It seems that wars will always be
because boys like to play war games.
Conflict gives some a joie de vivre,
and of that they should feel no shame.

7-1-06

Blessed are the peacemakers;
the bible says it's true.
The end might justify the means
when the war in the Mideast is through.
  With structured learning training
we should train our diplomats,
and brainstorm with Mideast students
letting them wear all sorts of hats.
  May each Mideastern city
have a sister city here,
that all retain humanity
a substitute for fear.
  Respecting Moslem religion and politics,
as good Americans should do,
indigenous systems of government
might become something better and new.
  Many may enjoy being pen-pals
writing back and forth,
learning about one another
East, West, South, and North.
  Americans seem to love slogans
on car bumpers and T-shirts.
Thinking up some of these
is likely to heal hurts.
  Alternatives to force
is what I'm attempting here.
Confusion of languages, I pray,
will just promote good cheer.

7-7-06

SLOGAN IDEAS:

Find Alternatives to Force
Children are the Future
Brainstorm Together
Improve Yourself
Get Grassroot Ideas
Diplomacy Works
The End Will Justify the Means
Jesus Will Justify
Have Humane Humility
Prosperity Proves Peace Is Power
Moslems Merit Manna Too
Imagine Islam Ideally
Imagine Christianity Ideally
Arbitrators Are Neutral
Half-breeds See As God Does
Good Cheer Combats Fear

7-13-06

I think what Iraq needs most
Is a big water park to boast.
The sound of water is holy to Moslems, you see;
So splashing on water slides would bring happiness at low fee.

7-17-06

Who should attempt to win the peace?
Should we wait until wars cease?
I think those who hate war,
and want peace like a dove to soar,
  such as those caught in the middle,
between feuding factions caring more than a little,
for example those half Moslem and half Jew,
or half Christian and half Moslem, there must be at least a few,
  and those maimed from weapons of war,
and those who have been made spiritually poor,
families and friends of these sorts,
and those who have been good sports,
  thru all the heartache and the pain,
and any who have love for the sound of rain,
should attempt to win the peace
whether before or after wars cease.

8-5-07

Jesus,
  May God guide Barack Obama.
May our country be ruled from God,
urban and rural people alike,
paper pushers and those turning sod.
  May Christians not fear politics too much,
and get our country on a good track,
ruled with Godly principles,
For diplomacy may we all have a knack,
  to negotiate peace and arbitrate
at every government level and in all homes too.
May the pride of the young be their strength*
in what they think, say, and do.
  May street smarts mean more than bullying
and more than fights for territory or position.
May the character of our young be good
and lead to demolition
  of anything ungodly or evil.
May our eyes be strong, healthy and good.
May our ears clearly hear God.
May our actions reflect God as they should.

*Bible: Proverbs 20: 29

2008

'Realists' from the 60's and 70's
think idealism is naïve;
that moral suasion is impractical
for implementing what we believe.
   Just as the U.S. never listened much
to minority nations in the U.N.,
'realists' think no one would listen to us
if we played mother hen.
   They think we must be policemen
of the whole world at large;
that respect we can only gain
via being a big fat barge.
   Right makes might
was taught us way back when.
Good foundations to build upon
must be strengthened once again.
   Self-discipline we need to learn
from Barack Obama, I think,
and from great Christian leaders
to rescue us from the brink
   of chaos caused of terror
and bully mentality on earth.
We need to stop tormenting one another
and learn to embrace good mirth.

1-30-09

The battleground of the ages
is the human mind.
Diplomats are the finest warriors
you could ever hope to find.
  Jesus is the greatest diplomat
who ever walked the Earth.
His death with pain and sorrow
was transformed into mirth,
  as He resurrected
into everlasting life above,
thus defeating evil.
The winner of all war is love.

6-17-09

CAPITALISM/COMMUNISM

  When supply is great
and demand is low,
prices will go down;
when supply is low
and demand is great,
high prices will make you frown.
  This is called
law of supply and demand,
that makes a free economy run;
if you efficiently use
resources and time,
your business will be a successful one.
  For certain things
demand is always high,
such as demand for food;
without such
you cannot live,
tho what you eat may depend on mood.
  For some things
mass-production works best,
and tho initial capital expense is great,
established businesses
can monopolize the market,
unless government changes fate.
  Our free-market economy
is based on the assumption
that self-interest leads to gain
for each and all
in society at large,
and big government is just a big pain.
  Communism,
on the other hand,
exults workers as head of state;
government determines wages and prices

according to use-value
being small or great.
  I was taught in the '70's
that communism
isn't efficient enough;
that long lines for items
cheap and in short supply
made shopping very tough.
  A planned economy
based on ideals
may be all well and good,
as long as we learn
from past mistakes,
and maintain as we should,
  what is worthwhile
about free market economies,
and not fold like the U.S.S.R.
Thus we may meet
human needs and rights.
Would our nation then go far?
  Brainstorming about
how to maintain the peace
without bombs being hurled,
is what political science is all about.
Keep dreaming of
living in a perfect world.
  Jesus taught us
to pray every day:
Thy Kingdom come.
We need to begin to imagine this Kingdom
so He won't find us all too dumb
  to implement
His verdicts and plans
exactly as He describes,
with love, understanding,
peace, and joy,
and indescribably good vibes.

7-17-09

IT TAKES ALL KINDS TO MAKE A WORLD

  If you believe in God, you believe in everything
I have heard it said.
Evil, I think, is gross disproportion
when there's too much hurt or dead.
  Some things that exist we may be better off without,
or at least we may think so,
when their numbers are too many,
or we consider them our foe.

7-18-09

How to use moral suasion
in our diplomacy with Iran?
Find humanity in their diplomats
before mentioning an atom-bomb ban.
  Identify with their frustration
in not getting real needs met the diplomatic way,
and use possibility thinking,
and really mean what you say.
  What are Iran's dreams
for itself in the world?
Why does it want military power
if it can gain good without any bombs hurled?
  How can we be Iran's friend
and make bombs irrelevant?
How can we show the way
and make governments less decadent?
  We can at least explain to Iran
that military might costs a lot;
that real wealth is more than that,
and some things cannot be bought.
  To break the cycle of coups d'etats
and power-mongers trying to rule,
historically the U.S. supports the status quo
and gets kids to go to school.

9-18-09

Moammar Gadhafi's message to the U.S.
was: 'own your mistakes',
tho the voice of his translator
did not mask his hates.
   Like nearly everyone, he likes Obama
with Obama's aura of goodness and respect,
that affords to all around
hope and real change effect.
   The media said Gadhafi rambled
from subject to subject without cohesion.
Tho that is somewhat true,
there is a very good reason:
   Their education was not the same
in content, methods, nor style.
Power was the end, not a means to an end
of pleasing people via going an extra mile.
   To be more like Obama
you must listen well;
be tolerant, not tormented,
giving ideas enough time to gel.
   When you act from a position of strength,
when ideas are firmly etched in your mind,
more power to you
and more responsibility you'll find.
   Then make it a point
to listen carefully to opposition,
so that you reach a consensus
and resentments don't reach fruition.

9-23-09

41

I guess bully mentality has always existed
shaping children's minds,
and war mentality is much the same thing
shaping ties that bind.
   Force is seem as obviously to be used
as the surest method to get your own way.
Power feels good to those who have it;
the weak need to have their say.
   With great power comes great responsibility
a wise person once said.
Resentments build up and multiply
when anyone gets maimed or dead.
   God is strong in weak people,
it is written somewhere;
so usually it's quite useful to listen
to those weaker, tho this seems rare.
   Negotiating from a position of strength
is the position most prefer to be in,
unless you are unwilling to use that force
and your adversaries are seeing.
   Bullying tends to beget bullies
as military action begets militants.
Diplomacy is for brilliant leaders,
negotiation is for willing participants.
   What could we learn from the Moslems?
I think to make use of arbitration,
when negotiation becomes deadlocked or heated
to help resolve fights between nations.

9-28-09

Self-interest of each leads to the good of all in a free-market economy.

Street-smarts is knowing how to get what you want, such as territory or position (via bullying, fighting, intimidating, manipulating, bonding, sharing . . .)

Bi-partisan government: Republicans say: 'Don't get sick, and if you get sick, die quickly.' Democrats say: Human rights for

all includes health. Republicans say: Classical economy of Adam Smith and trickle down. Democrats say: level the playing field.

Republic: Government of citizens via elected representatives and a president.

Democracy: Government of the people, via the people, and for the people.

Divine rule of kings: monarch rules via authority given him from God.

Altruism: valuing another person's needs or wants more than you value your own

Thy Kingdom come God : Father, Son, Holy Spirit

10-17-09

Foreclosed houses everywhere
and people who have no work,
too many spending what they do not have,
the economy has many quirks.
   Small businesses come and go.
Monopolies get bailed out.
Bankruptcies cost a lot.
In God many have grave doubt.
   I propose that a 4-day work-week
would get more people employed,
spreading wealth around
where needed bringing more joy.
   Entrepreneurs could be encouraged
to begin labor-intensive services
in industries where demand is high
so God's favor no one misses.
   All people are assets, not liabilities,
in our nation when God prevails.
Noone is expendable.
God never fails.
   When everybody tries their best
to serve God and humankind,
making the world a little better,
then lost sheep God finds.

10-29-09

Why fight in Afghanistan?
To give them a better life?
Can McChrystal be a McArthur,
creating good from war and strife?
   I'm not one to believe
in my country right or wrong,
tho I do believe in Obama,
and I wish for a better song.

   God, may we not gain new enemies
via battling against our foe.
Instead may we gain new friends.
Happy-go-luckily may we go.
   May we also gain understanding
between our drastically different cultures.
May our increased presence there
prove more than food for vultures.
   May some new industries thrive
to give Afghans more income too,
instead of drugs from poppies
bound to make people blue.

12-02-09

NATIONS   UPHOLD
HEAVEN   HOSTS   (who are)
PRAISING   GOD

4-10

"People are assets
not liabilities",
President Obama said.
Having him in office
is our big chance
to be spiritually fed.
   A person is more
than the sum of his parts
is a way of saying the same thing.
If we keep our faith
(God has no scarcity)
redemption He will bring.
   Our faith moves God.
Our need does not.
Miracles can happen now,
if we work real hard
to keep His Word
(the Bible tells us how).
   If we recognize
God's sovereignty and
His goodness, love, and power,
sooner or later
we'll reap rewards.
Blessings He will shower.
   If not in this life,
maybe in the one to come
God's justice we cannot see.
We must value our lives
for they belong to God
Let's just be content to be.

9-12-10

Do most diplomats love adversity?
Or do people wrongly attribute that?
It seems nothing gets accomplished
because of adversity crap.
  Dealing with pitfalls put in your path
takes time away from better things.
Someone as diplomatic as Obama
should be treated like a king.
  Just look at the health-care fiasco;
he listened respectfully to everyone.
Unfortunately, congress gave less respect.
I think that is quite dumb.
  What are people trying to prove?
That problems aren't to be taken seriously?
That diplomacy and negotiating are useless?
We should behave deliriously?
  Some of us don't have his skills.
I sure wish I did.
And I wish more people were more like him
so of demons we could be rid.

3-9-11

The best sort of congressman is the trustee sort—
the kind elected for his values and ideas.
He will use his brains, trust God and his gut
and be able to collaborate without fears—
    That maybe his constituents would do differently
if they were in his place,
or that maybe they won't re-elect him
nor give him any grace.
    Stubbornly sticking to a point of view
makes the issues be black and white.
Tho that may make his job easier,
a congressman should do what's right.
    To do what's right means you must listen
to differing points of view;
negotiate, debate, and change somewhat
to create good bills that are new.

3-9-11

In a society where rape is rampant
what is to be done?
If you are fearful, unstable, or weak,
learn martial arts for fun.
   Young girls remember
to love enemies as well.
so you won't be as traumatized;
if raped you'll live less hell.
   People of all ages learn
to be diplomatic, negotiate, arbitrate,
so as adults you'll find
better ways than rape.
   Government should not enforce
double standard laws
or there could be nothing left
except animals with claws.
   Remember in normal nature
females outnumber males,
when nature is out of sync
other issues pale.
   Double standard laws
make nature even more out of sync.
Women become more biologically upset
and we'd be brought to the brink (of chaos)
   If all people would be taught
some vocational skill,
then they could sustain their own homes
and life won't seem all uphill
   Cultivate in society
appreciation for the arts
as an expression of any emotion you have,
so that Cupid's darts
   won't seem so stupid and arbitrary
nor too selective nor too unfair,
because music, sculpture, and poetry
are better ways to share.

3-16-11

What constitutes a military mind?
At best it has good ethics and is stable.
At worst it is deranged and punitive,
or gleeful, taking all it is able.
   How do you foster stability
in a world where Satan exists?
Continually point out that God
can always defeat clenched fists.
   In a brain not functioning well,
that somehow does not seem true.
Losers usually seem to win,
and the Godly seem the proud and few.
   Those are people God uses as well
to reach his Godly ends.
Communication is key
as God's Kingdom He sends.
   Accidents happen
causing minds to be deranged.
Generational curses
are situations needing change.
   If communication is your gift,
communicating to such as these
in ways that stick in their memories
is sure to make God pleased.
   All people have a need for God
so if we communicate all He is,
and speak to their needs and desires,
they will want to be His.

6-9-11

Military science teaches what?
that man is basically greedy?
That power is an end and means to an end
so you and yours won't be needy?
 Man can be reasoned with
is what political science presumes.—
That we can reconcile our differences
when an attitude of respect each one assumes.
 Theology teaches us
God is sovereign over all.
Ethics and values are part of life too;
we each do our best to heed God's call.
 As long as wars and hate exist,
we can't all be always rational.
To be better than wild animals
we should bless God local, global, and national.

7-14-11

What does violence accomplish?
Radiation of hate,
generational curses,
cruel twists of fate.
What does non-violence accomplish?
Ridicule and scorn,
hope and love anew
after lives shattered and torn.
Who should live non-violence?
and who should live via the sword?
Should only the strong live at all?
For whom is Jesus Lord?
God is strong in our weakness,
so when you tried and think you failed,
He has a greater purpose;
your ship has not yet sailed.

7-25-11

Who should live non-violence?
Ones who can accomplish self-discipline
in the area of anger management
to conquer evil and sin.
  Who should live via the sword?
Those sinned against the most,
the capable of physical improvement
who are not inclined to boast.

7-25-11

Non-violence
should not be
passive-aggressive
so you see
if anger issues
you have inside
barely containable
that you hide,
choose rather to learn
the art of war
hand-to-hand combat
maybe blood and gore.
Reasonableness
you may learn
from political science
if you want to discern
what values you hold
close to your heart,
good reasons to fight
power to impart.
Faith in God
may help you too
and clean your blood
strengthening what you do.

7-26-11

If it is true that
you make your own luck,
how might I be lucky?
Choose not to pass the buck?
  On President Truman's desk it said:
"the Buck Stops Here".
So blame him for the Enola Gay
and enemies far and near?
  That seems pointless as
the man is dead and gone.
If I instead accept responsibility
with each new day that dawns,
  to better love my neighbors
and for God be salt and light,
curses may turn to blessings
and right may again make might.

7-26-11

If President Obama with his popularity
and his immense diplomatic skills,
could not accomplish much in office,
who <u>could</u> cure our country's ills?
   Christians have avoided politics
more than they do a dreaded disease.
How is it that our government says
we owe 14 trillion dollars in fees?
   Obviously we haven't prayed well enough
nor done enough concretely either.
Grassroot efforts should be enough
to pull our country together,
   if Christians aren't too lazy
and truly are light and salt
for our nation and for the world
so God does not find fault.

                                              8-31-11

In what way is legal abortion wrong?
Society's victims get victimized more.
The legal right to make a wrong decision
can multiply problems galore.
  The root of the problem being:
Why did you have sex?
Because you were needy
and under a hex?
  Why is it that
you could not trust God?
Under generational curses
daily you plod?
  Did you not understand
God required a leap of <u>faith</u>
for Him to trust <u>you,</u>
so you'd win His embrace?

9-4-11

INSPIRATION

GOOD =

> PLEASING
> UPHOLDING
> UPLIFTING
> ETHICAL
> JUSTICE
> PURPOSE
> IN ETERNITY

some requests:

  Inspire me, God,
to be enthusiastic with life;
to love with my heart,
not slice like a knife.
  Help me to connect
with goodness eyes to eyes
and to appreciate beauty
with less need for sighs.
  Give me good health, God,
and teach me your ways,
with good art and good music
for all of my days.
  Let me feel a sense of awe
in all I see of You.
Yet not my will, just thine be done
in all I seem and actually
am, and think, and say, and do.

  May I be a blessing, God.

8-15-05

HURRICANE KATRINA—IN FLORIDA

   Rustle, rustle, whoosh! the wind goes.
Trees bend and sway,
with an occasional snap
as a branch breaks away.
   I wonder if the trees
feel a rush;
like blood in our veins
does their sap gush?
   During the windstorm
the trees dance around,
making the wind audible
with whooshing, howling, whistling sound.
   Wet drops of rain,
pitter patter, splat, splat, splat,
give a new dimension
to this storm like that.
   The air is misty.
A big tree is knocked down.
The ground is soggy
all over town.
   Our power went out
in the midst of this storm,
due to a downed power line,
so darkness became the norm.

8-25-05

Puppy-love, I think,
is the best love there is;
joyful, trusting, happy-go-lucky,
emulated in show-biz.
And the rest of humanity too
tries to regain our youth,
copying what we notice
of God and love and truth.
God is love, the bible says,
and I think He loves this way.
So be ye as a little child
when you come to God each day.

6-18-06

Humility is said to be good,
while pride is said to be sin.
I'd like to see clearly the difference,
so I turn to God within.
   Humility gives glory to God,
while pride gives glory to self.
Pride has a glorious job,
Humility dusts a shelf.
   Pride is a show-off.
Humility does not flaunt.
Humility's in awe of God.
Pride, God does not daunt.
   Pride thrives on hype.
Humility loves peace.
Humility asks for little.
Pride's squeaky-wheel gets the grease.

   The pride of the young is their strength
says Proverbs twenty: twenty-nine:
Proof that pride can be good
so for glory days you'll pine.

1-28-09

God is awesome
in the Rocky Mountains
and on the windy,
rocky Maine coast.
   And in the midst
of South Florida hurricanes,
about Him
we've got to boast.
   God is gorgeous
in Japan
and in Afrique
de l'Ouest.
   I can't decide
where on Earth
He is at
His best.
   Europe has palaces
so grand,
where divine rule
of kings once reigned;
   and also museums
galore
where knowledge and culture
are gained.
   Different perspectives
and aspects of God
are distinct
in every place.
Thank You, Jesus Christ, for the goodness of God's Grace!

4-25-10

LOVE IS :

LIKE TO POINT OF JOY

HEART TO HEART CONNECT

EMOTION

5-10

MORE HUMBLE IS :

        QUIET
        RELAX
        NOT HYPE
        LISTEN
        CLOSE EYES
        FREEDOM FROM BUGS

6-1-10

"Let him who thinks he stands
take heed lest he fall"
says 1 Corinthians 10 : 12.
You with ears—heed God's call.
   Will power is not enough
to keep you from falling down.
God's grace is what you need,
in country, woods, city, or town.
   God is merciful, gracious, long-suffering,
and abounding in goodness and truth.*
So humble yourself as a little child should
and request forgiveness all you uncouth.

*book of Exodus 34 : 6 (Bible)

                                                    6-11-10

Bible recommended: My motives and purposes being—edify and be full of Christ's love—I ernestly desire via divine Spirit: (1 Corintians 12 : 7-11)

Have wisdom and put wisdom into good words; express wisdom in good ways.
Edify with useful knowledge I have; and edify with useful knowledge I attain.
Have good faith.
Heal needy of healing.
Put supernatural instantaneous power to good uses, (good miracles).
Speak from mind of God, (prophesy).
Good discernment of spirits.
Speak tongues.
Interpret tongues.

(I pray for good timing, good sequence, good duration of all and good placing)

My part in attaining the above: according to and in proportion to the grace I am given:
(Romans 12 : 3-8)

Minister.
Teach.
Advise, encourage, (exhortation).
Give liberally.
Lead diligently.
Mercy.
Love without hypocrisy.
Abhor evil, cling to good.
Kindly affectionate.
Spirit fervent, diligent.

6-24-10

MALE   VERSUS   FEMALE

- We're more alike than we are different.
- There's a little bit of man in every woman and a little bit of woman in
  every man.
- Biological differences.
- Psychological preferences.
- Chemical attractions (animal magnetism).
- Cultural stereotypes.

Traditionally female:
Dress-up, tea party, house, jumprope, dolls, make-up, sewing, cooking, dresses,
skirts, ruffles, bonnets, high heels, long hair, slower, emotional, receptive,
intuitive, submissive, shorter, fatter, more stamina, nurturer, softer.

Traditionally male:
Trucks and cars, guns, hunting, sports, fishing, camping, boats, pants, neckties,
caps, short-hair, faster, intellectual, initiator, spiritual head of household,
protector, provider, taller, leaner, stronger-muscles.

Behind every good man is a good woman.

Only Spartan women give birth to real men.

Spartan means living frugally with minimal things.

Sparta was a city-state in Greece with the best warriors.

7-2-10

71

Life is fragile
handle with prayer.
God holds us all
in His good care.
It might not seem so
at this time.
Have good faith.
God is sublime.
With God's help
you can do
super things;
yes it's true.
Maybe not
what you planned.
Better yet
with God's hand.
Talk to God;
He's your friend.
Just like a tree,
it's good to bend
towards the glorious
Son above,
reflecting always
God's great love.

With God all things
are possible.
Jesus makes them
probable.

Have a good day.

9-7-10

Zedekiah Jesus,
You are just what I need—
ensuring that God is mighty and just
while saving us indeed
   Your personality I'd like to know more,
Your likes and dislikes and such,
so that I can better please you;
I want your love so much.
   Glimpses of Your love I have had.
There's surely more I can say and do,
to have Your love encompass me
with Your motley crew.
   Zedekiah Jesus,
be Yourself for us.
You've overcome the world;
help us to not fuss
   about our daily lives
that we have got to live.
Help us all learn to love,
and want and know how to give.
   Zedekiah Jesus,
You are the best, while humble.
How You manage that, I don't know.
I'm so prone to stumble.
   Zedekiah Jesus,
May Your glory always shine.
May goodness be contagious.
May I be refined.

9-16-10

How to be just poor, not devastated:

  Have stamina
and be physically fit,
so walking and laboring
won't bother you a bit.
  Be adaptable
to people and place.
Be friendly and have
a likeable face.
  Know where and how
to get basic needs met.
Barter well,
and you'll be set.
  Enjoy ghetto art
and simple sounds
such as gutter water gurgling
under the ground.
  Have a good dream
you are aiming for.
If you are kind and helpful,
you can be happy for sure.

10-12-10

If you find you aren't
some of these things,
cry out to God
'till angels earn their wings.

Bear your cross
and learn to cope.
In yourself and others
stir up faith and love and hope.

10-16-10

How much do I really love Jesus?
is the question to ask ourselves tonight;
inspired in Friday-night prayer group,
seeking to make things right.
   I know I really love God
very, very, much.
Jesus is His reflection
who bestows love and such,
   on us who may not deserve it;
tho we can and should appreciate
all that God has done for us.
Jesus is first-rate.
   When Jesus was new to this world,
he was awesome, indeed.
His way of teaching was unique,
with analogies of sowing seed.
   Simple, pure, and true
His words are still today.
Many cannot relate,
tho Jesus is the way.
   He has been a stumbling block
to those who close their hearts.
Just open up and let Him in;
God's love He'll then impart.
   Be ye as a good little child
when you're in need of God the most,
humbling yourself as a little child should,
and about Him you'll want to boast.
   For He is able to mighty things,
things even greater than way back when
via any person that He chooses,
and He's coming back to us again.

12-17-10

76

God is the ultimate multi-tasking boss.
He focuses completely on infinity of issues.
He perfectly, intimately, knows each and all.
He has infinite patience and time for anything.
He communicates to any who want to hear.
There is nothing He cannot do.
He loves humankind very much.

Thank You, God for all You are and do.
Thank You for being complete.
Thank You for being eternal.
Thank You for being all we need You to be.
Thank You for saving souls.
Thank You for healings in soul, mind, heart, emotion, spirit, and body.
Thank You for loving us.
Thank You for all You give to us.
Thank You for knowing everything.
Thank You for being everywhere.
Thank You for Jesus Christ.
Thank You for life.
Thank You for the Earth.
Thank You for all creation.
Thank You for music and art.
Thank You for stories.
Thank You for poetry.
Thank You for Your Word.

1-3-11

What causes, I wonder,
chemical attractions to go askew
and makes you desire people
not good for you?
   -Natural affections
in families lacking;
- homosexual marriages
getting legal backing . . .
   Why isn't maternity
'the most loving option'?
Why does Rumplestiltzken
favor adoption?
   Grafting branches for fruit
on a different type of tree
does not often work best
unfortunately,
   for the branch grafted on
tho both trees may yet thrive;
 (If you're a tree, I guess,
you don't need to wive.)
   Maybe you can spare
a branch or two
so that your neighbor
feels less blue.
   Mother and child together
is naturally the best way.
Wanna-be adopters
should make both more okay.
   Serve as governess, for example,
or as a handyman.
Mentoring mothers
is making a better stand.

1-12-11

Don't give up on God.
He'll never give up on you.
When it seems God is hateful or fickle,
What, then, should you do?
Remember it's the blood of Jesus
That lets you reach God at all.
Humble yourself to receive love
Because He'll answer your call.

3-20-11

If a good tree can't bear bad fruit,
and a bad tree can't bear good,
only Jesus can be saved—
not any from our neighborhoods.
   Your parents would have to be good
and descended from a long line of such,
for you to attain heaven,
for God to like you much.

   Jesus is the answer
for the world today;
above Him is the Father
Jesus is the way.

3-21-11

Respect all people.
Honor the best.
Worship God.
Have God's rest.
Quell aggravation.
Edify your neighbor.
Assert what is right.
Win God's favor.
Be like a beacon.
Light the way.
Be like salt.
Season each day.
Have good faith.
Be like a rock.
Live your life.
Watch your talk.
Smile if you like.
Laugh if you feel.
Gripe if you must.
Love being real.

3-28-11

Is God a hard taskmaster,
expecting the most of you,
testing you at your most vulnerable
so you fail each test you do?
   Or is He a loving Father
trying to mold you into something good,
accepting you always, wherever you're at,
hoping you'll do as you should?

   When trust is complete,
yours in Him, and His in you,
He becomes that loving Father
making life good in all you do.

3-29-11

Is oxygen a scarce resource?
Who regulates its allocation?
   I want plenty of it—
more than I've been rationed.
   Oxygen to my brain
would help me remember better.
   Oxygen to my blood
would make me a go-getter.
   Oxygen to my heart
would make me feel more joy.
   Oxygen everywhere
would get me to be employed.

                                                        4-8-11

What plants produce the most oxygen?

What stimulates breathing?

Don't treat me like machinery,
dysfunctional in some part,
poking, probing, analyzing, testing;
that's not good for my heart.
   Don't treat me like a criminal,
rotten to the core,
judging, rejecting, gossiping, hating me,
shutting every door.
   Don't treat me like a sicko,
diseased and contagious too,
shunning ostracizing, quarantining me,
I've got the alienation blues.
   Just treat me like a friend in Christ
trusting God to protect you and me.
God is all-knowing, all-powerful, everywhere.
He wants to make all people free.

4-25-11

A Christian perspective on suffering
is that suffering builds your soul,
gaining fortitude, perseverance, gratitude,
whatever is God's goal.
   Some people learn compassion,
others learn tolerance.
Most learn to rely on God
for their deliverance.
   To each has been given
a measure of faith;
admit it and use yours well.
God can build you up, even if your faith
is smaller than Tinkerbell.

The French have a saying:
"You must suffer to be beautiful"
Not all suffering leads to beauty, tho,
so consider your blessings plentiful.
   I pray for good timing and durations of pains,
that they lead to a greater good,
for those adversely affected
in every place and neighborhood.
   God always provides a way out
of situations too bad for you.
You don't get more than you can handle.
God's love is true.

4-25-11

Some qualities of soul are:
Integrity
Faith
Love
Fortitude
Perseverence
Gratitude
Tolerance
Compassion
Empathy
Mercy
Diligence
Giving
Edifying
Wisdom
Discernment
Patience
Reverence

4-25-11

What is respectable?
Strong eyes
Position of authority
Health
Wealth
Well-kept appearance
Strong blood
Confidence
Being considerate
Strength of mind and body
Skills and abilities
Positive attitude
Attentiveness
Appreciativeness
Being law-abiding
Effort
Goodness
Authenticity
Caring
Good deeds
Common sense
Diligence, stamina
Wisdom
Savoir faire
Good manners
Diplomacy
Beauty
Achievements, accomplishments
Reverence

5-12-11

How to practice giving respect:

Experience receiving respect
Develop respectable qualities
Don't judge
Find good qualities in others
Be sensitive to other's feelings

5-13-11

What is reverence?

Respect for God
In awe of God
Love for God and for creation
Spiritual discipline
Gratitude

5-12-11

How to age well:

Love and respect older people
Prefer young
Be authentic
Be around those who love you
Keep your mind active
Converse, communicate
Do what you enjoy
Eat, exercise, dress well
Have God's favor

5-16-11

When did God seem weak to me?
When disobedience did abound,
When faith the size of a mustard seed
Was not rooted on solid ground.
   So make a joyful sound unto God,
To praise, thank, worship, and uplift.
That is what the angels do;
Aren't we meant to do more than drift?
   Also, prayer mobilizes angels
To act on God's behalf.
God is moved via our faith, not our need,
So in the face of danger—laugh, praise, pray, thank, worship, skip, dance,
run, sing, or uplift any other way you are able as
Holy Spirit lets.

5-17-11

How to stop new problems
from being added to the old,
compounding or multiplying,
horrors to unfold?
  Believe in God;
don't give up on Him.
Learn to pray well;
use words at God's whim.
  Spread the word
that God is good.
Love your neighbors
as you should.

5-23-11

God does not will that any should perish;
He wills that all shall find redemption in Jesus.*
How can we avoid expediency
so God's favor frees us?
  All things work to the good
for those who love God true;
meaning noone is expendable and
if you love God He'll bless you.
  Are some people unable
to be good for others?
God says: no, that negativity
is part of life—ask your mothers.
  She who lives via the sword
shall via the sword be slain,
unless she becomes a mother—
proof she's forgiven; love is gained.
  Does it ever happen
that one must die that others may live?
Jesus taught so with his sacrifice;
He wants us also to learn to give.
  Valuing our lives
above all else is right.
Jesus cleanses from all sin
become blameless in His sight.

*Bible: 2 Peter 3:9

5-24-11

93

When does God want one to lay down his life?
When he's old and worn-out, I think.
When he's not good for himself anymore
When most anything drives him to drink.
  When communication is lacking
Between new generations and him
When he has no mate who will miss him
When his smile is weak and grim
  When there's no chance of him singing
From his heart, somehow:
"I was so much older then,
I'm younger than that now."

  Kids keep you young
Love keeps you alive
God is your friend
Relating makes you jive.

The family that possesses an old person possesses a treasure.

5-25-11

A child who won't obey
needs to learn reverence.
God can teach him that
when he needs deliverance.
  If he is open to God,
bring him soon to church.
Let good servants of God mentor him,
and scriptures let him search,
  so he grows in respect and love.
For God may he be in awe,
learning spiritual discipline
and gratitude for the law.
  Fellowship amongst believers too,
eating and having good fun,
pleases God much
as we learn to follow the Son.

6-2-11

People who live
in houses of glass
should not throw stones?
Don't be crass.
  The vulnerable
are more likely to see,
and critique better
than the power-hungry.
  Also, houses of glass
likely are made
of bullet-proof substance
of top grade.

6-17-11

A genius is a person having great mental capacity and inventive ability.

The genius of one generation is the common sense of the next.

Genius is common sense to an uncommon degree.

Genius is 1% inspiration and 99% perspiration.

Who is a genius in the opinions of the young generation?

What should geniuses put their brains to studying?

What work, jobs, employment is for geniuses?

6-30-11

What is selfishness indicative of?
Neediness unfulfilled?
Contrary reactions to others' demands?
Brain cells that have been killed?
  Each person should know his own self best.
What is most conducive to that?
(instead of causing disproportionate greeds
and side-effects such as fat).

7-12-11

Making good of bad situations,
Seemingly enjoying adversity,
may make you rise above the crowd
who resent you with animosity.

7-14-11

Speaking the truth in love means what?
Being sure the other person feels loved,
when saying something honest (tho maybe hurtful)
as you are guided from God above.

7-17-11

When the bible speaks of fruits,
to what does it refer?
To results of the Word in your life;
over works, fruits God prefers.
  Works may be vain efforts;
fruits are something produced.
With help of the holy spirit,
fruits for God may be loosed.

(nobody can do nothing as good as I can?)

7-17-11

Making evil a requirement
for getting gains from your pains,
is modern-day idiocy
that promotes the draining of brains.
God is all-knowing, all-powerful, everywhere.
Satan just cannot win.
When all humanity realizes this,
Jesus can remove all sin.
Minds fresh and new seldom need hard knocks
to enable them to leam hard things.
The sinned against become sinners too.
I pray Jesus our redemption brings.
Clinging to our savior brings a greater good
when clinging isn't all you do.
Faith without works is dead, the bible says.
May we all be fruitful too.

7-21-11

Evil makes you ugly.
Being angry makes you loud.
Neither makes you stronger—
Just wispy like a cloud.

Putting God first is real beauty.
Seeing beauty in the crass is good.
Strength comes from your integrity;
endurance from doing as you should.

7-21-11

Since hate tends to feed upon itself,
should it not be talked about?
How does love best assert itself?
How can we give God more clout?
  Anger needs outlets for expression.
Words are an effective way.
On a release anger track forever, tho,
cannot be best, I say.
  Garbage in, garbage out,
I have heard that said.
How may I communicate
pleasant things to and from my head?
  Music and songs that uplift me
Are the primary things I've found.
I love people to write and sing
Keeping feet solid on the ground.

7-22-11

When should I say "I love you"?
When I see something in the person that I love?
When I feel the emotion myself?
When I know the person won't feel shoved?
When I need the person to love me?
When I sense the person needs my love?
When the person says "I love you" first?
When driven from God above?

I think you shouldn't often say it,
especially when not feeling it true;
nor when the person's not reciprocating
and the situation doesn't favor you.

"Thank you for loving me",
is good when you can't reciprocate
the love a person says they feel for you
for turmoil to abate.

7-22-11

God, I thank you for loving me.
I want to love you well,
And reflect well upon You too,
Your best aspects to tell.

7-22-11

Don't keep me on the straight and narrow.
Instead make the straight and narrow more broad,
via being salt and light to the world
until every person reveres almighty God

7-2-11

<u>Light</u>:

brightens
brings joy
allows seeing
gives warmth
feeds plants
brings understanding
eliminates darkness
causes: insight
                 ingenuity
                 inventiveness
                 intuition
                 imagination
                 integrity
                 initiative
Is: glorious
      lustrous
      shimmering
      sparkling
      effervescent
      reflecting
      lovely
      radiant
      shining

7-26-11

What is the glory of God?
Splendor of our king.
Victory of righteousness.
Favor of heaven we sing.

7-26-11

What are qualities of a good teacher? Good teachers:

1) Begin with teaching basics; don't presume knowledge; build a foundation for skills development.
2) Help students remember what they've learned; make knowledge attaining memorable and enjoyable.
3) Encourage, advise, edify.
4) Are personable and likeable
5) Include everyone in the class.
6) Are acquainted with various learning styles, adapting to each student.
7) Genuinely like people, particularly the group they're teaching, e.g. kids.
8) Are genuinely interested in the subject matter themselves.
9) Enjoy sharing what they know.
10) Continue to improve and learn themselves.

8-4-11

Jesus came to me
in my backyard one day,
as a little boy
as I was soaking in sun rays.
  God exists in nature too,
and He caused me to think:
Jesus as little boy
is like a missing link
  between mothers and God.
Was nothing written that Jesus said—
to His folks while growing up,
while being nurtured and fed?

8-7-11

Why should anyone want
to have more than a billionaire?
Aristocracy lacking divine right to rule
needs to learn how to care.
   If we had an assets ceiling
of one billion dollars or so,
small businesses could compete
so we'd all feel much less woe.

8-14-11

Who do I say that God is?
God is a being of love,
awesome in scope and ability,
everywhere and reigns from above.
   God is pure spirit and heart,
who loves to commune with us—
a just and merciful savior,
raising us up from our daily fuss.
   God is strong and mighty,
going against all errors and wrongs,
making good from what's not,
putting each person where he belongs.
   God is perfection personified,
incomprehensible, for sure;
making simple humans
have hearts that are more pure.

8-17-11

I wonder what's been recalculated,
and what was originally planned
in my life past, present, and future;
I'd like to see clearly God's hand.

8-26-11

How to make an economy out of chaos:
do something that's worthwhile.
make things or serve somebody;
go the extra mile.
   Honor a form of currency
or many forms besides cash;
practice bartering as well;
other cultures do not bash.
   Charity begins at home,
so buy American-made.
Give to victims who live close-by;
make sure your employees get paid.
   Support local businesses
more than oligopolies.
If you have no skills in demand,
go to school and get degrees.
   If you have a billion dollars,
and business is easy for you,
mentor other people
so they can do what you do.
   Have integrity always.
Give your whole self to God,
via loving God and people.
Respect His holy temple, your bod.

8-27-11

Cloudy, rainy, day
drizzling sadly.
Water vapor
reflecting sun
shining into my eyes,
dazzling, bright,
Godlike.

8-30-11

God,
  Pray with my eyes closed,
You reminded me today.
I'm writing so I'll remember
what You had to say.
  Discernment is also important.
I pray that I'll learn this too;
when to think my prayers
in concepts or words to You.
  When to whisper, also,
and when to pray aloud.
When jubilant, I likely will yell
alone or in a crowd,
  to give honor to You
who are so glorious.
You make life worth living,
when You are mindful of us.

8-31-11

Trying to get to heaven
via the works You do,
is like filthy rags,
useless to God and to you.
When Holy Spirit leads you
(as that proves to God you have faith)
good works will naturally result
via you for the human race.

9-12-11

I think the 700 club
is a disgrace to TBN
unsupportive of President Obama
and bashing Islam time and again.
   Hate monger of a bad sort
I think Pat Roberson is.
Typical old republican,
at diplomacy he's not a wiz.
   He's got beady eyes and growly speech;
I can forgive him that—
if he personally converts a Moslem extremist,
and mentors him to sit where he (Pat) sat.

   Jesus, please forgive me
for hatred in my heart.
I do not know his story;
wisdom please impart.
   Wars leave residues
of hatred for a long time.
Where an ounce of prevention is worth a pound of cure
please send miracles, wonders, and signs.
   With power comes responsibility;
TBN has a loud voice,
all over the world; politically,
may they make a better choice.

9-13-11

What I would like to see on the 700 club:

1) missionaries working to convert Moslems to Christianity
2) missionaries recruiting more missionaries
3) appreciation shown to those who are missionaries
4) victory stories of victims of hate crimes, who overcame their troubles.

  Can God create generations
with very many missionaries,
and peace-Corps volunteers,
and diplomatic dignitaries,
  enough to overcome
the ill-effects of wars
with the conflicting ideologies?
Can He open doors?
  It seems to me <u>all</u> humanity
needs to do our part,
having concern for all creation
and giving God our whole heart.

9-15-11

God,
Please make me be a good new creation.
I give You all of me.
Keep anything You want.
Eliminate all debris.

9-25-11

There's gotta be a little Sunshine Sometimes

  There's got to be some sunshine
to warm your heart and soul;
some kindness and some friendliness
we fulfill that role,
  for one another as Christians
drawing strength from God too;
love is our battle-cry;
we're salt and light in what we do.
  God's directives are quite simple:
come to God; go to the world; give;
love God and love people;
share and truly live.

10-26-11

ISSUES

If it is true that to all
a measure of faith has been given,
and God won't give more than you can handle,
why does it seem I am driven-
    to fail each test He gives me,
tho I continually try my best
at everything I endeavor to do,
yet my life seems such a mess?
    Time heals all wounds, it's been said,
and I think that it is true,—
God's way of doing a miracle
anonymously for you.
    Problems do compound sometimes
so before old problems go away,
new ones might be added,
so I wonder: where's God today?
    God is the almighty one,
so there's nothing He can't do.
He healed us 2000 years ago.
It's just got to be received in you.

    Is testing the root of all evil?
Beginning with Adam and Eve?
Is a seed of doubt inherent in every test?
causing us to disbelieve?
    Please give me not any surprise quizzes, God;
I never liked those too well.
May I be prepared to serve you
May I have a joyous testimony to tell.

2-9-09

125

When is it best to follow your heart?
any time Cupid throws his dart?
isn't that quite arbitrary?
Is that always the one you should marry?
  The heart wants what the heart wants?
Against good common sense your prize you'll flaunt?
I don't want to intellectualize every thing;
Tell me my heart great joy can bring.
  Cupid rarely sends his darts my way
unlike when I was a teen—then every day—
randomly for many guys.
Cupid is powerful for his size.

9-17-10

A man after God's own heart
the Bible says King David was.
King David lets his heart instruct him
in all he says and does.
   His heart was selfish and he stole
a wife from Uriah, a Hittite man.
He had Uriah killed, so from God's presence
you'd think David would be banned.
   God kept giving David more chances
to do the things good in God's sight.
Tho David messed up, he was true to God
and desired to deserve God's might.
   I think God saw in him a little boy,
the youngest son in Jesse's brood of eight,
who tended sheep and played the harp,
and had dreams of becoming great.

9-17-10

Do you prefer to entertain or be entertained?
is a question I was once asked.
I prefer to be entertained
is the response I came up with fast.
   He gave me a look of disgust or disapproval,
I yet am unsure why.
I think, honestly, everyone prefers
to be entertained, tho some lie.
   Those truly able to entertain
must be able to entertain themselves first,
or others will not enjoy them,
and the result is they will feel cursed.
   It's been said that bringing happiness to others
brings happiness to yourself as well.
So your own happiness is your yardstick
as to how well your entertaining should sell.

11-14-10

God, is the internet evil?
Or do some just see it that way?
I think it's only bad when it replaces You
in the lives of many these days.
   It seems to me that many feel
they're in a war or contest against You;
that to be openly on Your side is stupid;
that the Godly are the proud and few.
   Because obviously the internet is here to stay,
just like airplanes are;
and it cannot be avoided
nor admired from afar.
   I'm not technologically minded.
Computers aren't easy for me to use.
It would help if technology were not at war
with religion and people would choose
   to do unto others now and then,
as they would have done unto them,
before they, themselves, are in dire need
of Jesus, the crème de la crème.

3-9-11

What can make you feel alienated:
- rejection
- being a third wheel
- feeling shy
- lacking initiative
- being a foreigner
- being different
- medical problems—eyes, blood, fat, breathing . . .
- anger issues
- lack of good communication
- being misnamed
- lack of solid foundation in God
- not relating
- self-reliance
- being a lab project, not a pet
- being outnumbered—the minority viewpoint
- having a disability

3-26-11

With Jesus as lord of my life, what is expected of me?
1) love God with all my heart, soul, mind, and strength
2) love my neighbor as myself
3) pursue what is good for myself and for all
4) be salt and light
5) pray with good words and sincerity
6) listen to God
7) revere God
8) respect people
9) honor God's servants
10) give

3-29-11

What do Pharisees expect:
1) obey them
2) keep house immaculate
3) vote Republican
4) be nice
5) discern well
6) be not provoked
7) be stylish
8) don't fart
9) work
10) smile

3-31-11

Uprooting what is planted
serves what good purpose, when?
When tomato plants get too big for their flats,
you transplant them into pots big enough for them.
 Then, when they're a little bigger,
you plant them in the field,
where they can grow as big as they'll get,
and their fruits they will yield.
  You might put up stakes, so they grow tall,
and will not rot on the ground.
Pick the tomatoes when they're not quite ripe.
Put them on window sills where sunlight abounds.

  Are people like tomato plants
that benefit from being transplanted?
Or does that drive us crazy?
Who has raved and ranted?
  Just me? Or most people?
Just the unsound? Or just the old?
Just those from warm climates?
Or just those from the cold?

4-11-11

133

Who are the real care-givers?
Any who bring love and fun
to those who have some dysfunction.
They are the only ones.
    It's good to make life comfortable, of course,
and someone's got to do the tedious stuff.
When that's all said and done,
it's really not enough.
    Holy spirit can brighten your days
if you have even just a spark.
Be sure to enlighten the clueless
that they keep you from the dark.
    I couldn't handle urine, vomit, and poop,
every single day as an aide.
Nor deal with imnmobility or bedsores
and keeping the beds all made.
    I've been a PCA before,
so I know this is true of me.
I dislike being depressed,
and that's what I would be.
    As a patient, I looked forward to
occupational therapy,
(a medical term for arts and crafts).
It broke the tedium for me.
    I also liked the field trips,
walking in parks and such.
Jobs doing those things I might like.
Nothing else medical much.

4-18-11

What sort of dysfunctioned person
would complement me well?
(so, like Jack Sprat and his wife*
we'd keep each other out of hell).
    Could I quell the fears of the fearful?
Or break the obsessive out of their ruts?
Or help those with feelings of unreality?
Or bandage those with cuts?

*nursery rhyme:
"Jack Sprat could eat no fat.
His wife could eat no lean.
So between them both, you see,
they licked the platter clean."

4-19-11

Some psople think they want
more suffering in their lives,
because they feel nothing.
For soul they need to strive.
   The lack of pain, I think,
Is a form of suffering, too.
Embrace what you do not like
about your life, so blue.
   Creating problems for yourself,
or for others you think need pain,
you might regret in the future.
In Jesus find your gain.

4-24-11

When I got baptized Baptist,
my understanding was far from complete.
I feel it still is now;
the devil we must defeat.
  Is baptism like a Christening
where you get your name?
Does it cleanse you from <u>all</u> sin?
Does it make you better, not the same?
  Does it mean you died with Jesus,
and arose with Him anew?
Does it lead you to destruction
unless you are one of the very few?
  Is it good for babies
in case they die too soon?
Does it ensure their way to heaven?
Is it a great boon?
  Must you be not ignorant
of all that it entails?
Must you truly repent first?
Is it primarily for males?
  Is it only real
if you got immersed?
If you were only sprinkled,
then are you cursed?
  Should you only get baptized once?
is it okay to be baptized again?
Must it be in the ocean?
Does it matter what denomination you're in?
  Jesus got baptized of John
because He wanted to do everything right.
Did Jesus teach a <u>new sort</u> of baptism?
are Christians right in God's sight?

4-25-11

He or she who is without sin, make the first judgmental comment.

He or she who is without flaw, give the first analytical test.

He or she who is without vulnerability, enforce the sodomy and double standard laws first.

He or she who is without a trace of the opposite sex in their being, define who is male and who is female.

If, in an imperfect world, you want to be a judge or analyst, try to treat your lab specimens as normally as possible, with minimal technology, and natural environ-ments. If they act weird, change your methods of gaining info.

Try not to warp your specimen's mind; that is, don't keep giving negative reinforcements of the same sort when you see physical or other manifestations of negativity over a course of time.

Mind, and body, and spirit, and emotion, and soul are all connected. When your lab rat gets mean after you've ground dirt into a sore a dozen times, you don't need to continue grinding dirt into that sore. You know what the effect is.

The mind reacts the same way to negativity into its sore spots.

So bugs please stop calling me 'boy'. You know it aggravates. Also, society has plenty of sexual deviants already (resulting from diverse cultures intermingling with separate stereotypes of what constitutes male, and what constitutes female -besides the obvious biological, physical differences). I tell you, I'm female, adult, and mother of a 19 year old son. Grow up, get some respect and stop bugging.

4-25-11

Why do little boys want to be
police or firemen when they grow up?
So they can be the boss
and drive a shiny car or truck?
And why do they continue
to want to grow up for that?
So they can be loud and obnoxious
and be nobody's doormat?
If their heart is truly good,
they just want to protect
what is dear to people
so the future won't be wrecked.

4-30-11

When, if ever, is gross disproportion
a very <u>good</u> thing?
When great masses of people
go to hear Tina Turner sing?
   When Jesus and his disciples
heal the sick and the lame?
When martyrs die for truth
with or without fame?
   Is gross disproportion
often very bad?
Like when suffering makes you grotesque?
or just a passing fad?

5-1-11

Secular USA

   Is there no point in going to school?
Or do people just miss the point?
After going to school faithfully, you may burn out quick,
and end up sick or in the joint.
   If you're sick, you must work with the sick;
it seems there's not another future for you.
If you're a criminal you learn to work with your hands,
and get factory work to do.
   If your parents were labeled bad or sick,
you likely will be worse,
unless God helps you to overcome.
In the process you may feel cursed.
   If your parents were never labeled at all,
you must fight "nothing's wrong with you".
As others grope at you for salvation,
you'll feel worse than they do.
   Anyone who overcomes the odds
will be fattened up for the slaughter.
It's hard to see and advantage, then,
to being called God's son or daughter.
   Witnesses have been persecuted much
over the course of time.
As for me, I prefer to be at home,
making up poems that rhyme.

5-12-11

141

Once upon a time, in the days of ancient Greece and Rome, mini gods and goddesses sat on mini-thrones.

God almighty watched, while most were ignorant then, of His existence guiding women and men.

Some were merchant people, shipping goods from port to port. They used stars to guide them. They were not bad sorts.

The stars they made into pictures, to remember the star positions. For fun, stories were made up about them, reflecting people's volitions.

5-14-11

This is Cupid's story: Cupid is a little boy angel who has fun shooting arrows into people's hearts, making them fall in love.

People honor Cupid on Saint Valentine's Day with cards, hearts, chocolates, and flowers, given to loved ones. Cupid is a good angel whom almighty God mobilizes when we pray to almighty God. The name, Cupid, rhymes with stupid, so Cupid sometimes feels insecure about himself. God loves Cupid, and Cupid loves God.

So how did it come about that sometimes people fell in love with persons wrong for them? Did people worship Cupid and other angels, gods, and goddesses to their detriment? I think so. The stars and planets, in fixed positions, said to represent the gods' personalities, also were said to determine people's personalities.

Asteroids have destroyed the planet Pluto in the modern age of Aquarius (when peace is guiding the planets and love is steering the stars). Pluto had been "god of the underworld" and was considered somewhat sinister. Perhaps Pluto got a hold of some of Cupid's arrows. I don't know.

Supposing it was Pluto who misused Cupid's arrows (causing men to fall in love with men and causing women to love the study of astrology to their detriment) what then transpired in the heavens?

God sent His son, Jesus, from heaven to earth, as a baby born to a virgin woman named Mary. Jesus was God's mouthpiece and example, who lived a perfectly sinless life on earth and spoke vehemently against sodomy, and against astrology, and against powers and principalities affecting humans. He preached love for almighty God, and love for people. He was humble and kind and devoted to God. Jesus taught us to pray to our Father in heaven: (almighty God who is all-knowing, all-powerful, and present everywhere. He is truth, love, light, life, and good. He is eternity and infinity). We may ask of God anything in Jesus' name. God is creator and preserver of all, and He loves what He makes.

Jesus' words were recorded in a book called the bible, for us to know and love God better. It has been translated into hundreds of languages and dispersed worldwide. So we may read it, discuss it, and proclaim it. It's awesome.

5-24-11

Humor at its best is harmless.
When done in love, it is that.
Finding humor in hardship can be a defense
that God may have to combat.
   When something makes you laugh,
because it's just very funny,
you'll know it comes from God
if it saved you from feeling crummy.

5-17-11

UNLESS:
it's sneering, snubbing, gloating, cursing, impulsive, or contrived?

God is everywhere, and all things work to the good for those who love
God . . .

even Mafia?

even Satan himself?

even me?

5-21-11

The ultimate turnoff
is the smoking of cigarettes,
done with spite not love,
or do I fuss and fret
  over something minor?
Do smokers just not think
enough about what they're doing?
Don't they drive the world to the brink
  of chaos sooner or later?
Of misery far too much?
Woe is a part of life too, you say?
It comes naturally, you such and such.
  Because man is a finite creature,
also families aren't best for all,
and everyone can't be in the best place always,
so people are bound to fall.
  At least try to do good;
life is more than a game
of trying to destroy everyone
while extending the game just the same.

6-1-11

What in my life today prevents me from making money?
What do I need to do to be gainfully employed?

Do I have a good reputation?
Do I make a good first impression?
Do I converse well?
Do I have the needed skills for the job?
Am I responsible?
Am I trainable?
Am I likeable?
Can I improve my employability? How?
From whom should I get feedback?

6-9-11

Reasons for smoking cigarettes that I've heard:
- calms your nerves
- kills your appetite
- wards off mosquitoes and expensive chicks
- looks cool
- you don't want to live to be old
- something to do
- you can use them as cash

Reasons to not smoke cigarettes:
- bad for your health
- bad for the health of people around you
- Satan worship
- the body is the temple of the Holy Spirit.
- addictive
- looks repulsive
- expensive

7-4-11

What can make a person ugly and dull?
Drudgery, poverty, and pain.
These also can make a person like a leach
sucking blood for all his gain.
   Misery seems to beget more misery
even when you appreciate what you've got.
Tho love may be blind and retarded,
it's the best way to get the gains you've sought.
   Give a little more than you're asking them for,
then your love will turn the key,
may seem naïve and stupid;
at any rate it keeps you free.
   Tho easy like Sunday morning
may get taken advantage of,
good things may land in your lap
as God rules from above.
   Honestly, I haven't loved others
the way I would want to be loved.
It's incapacity, I guess.
Maybe I need a shove
   in the direction of mutual gains,
away from negative ruts.
If that is somehow possible,
I would trust my guts.

7-8-11

If everyone was Christian,
and there were not any Jews,
would Old Testament Law be forgotten
In favor of the latest news?

7-14-11

Why do good people join the military?
Personal power gives them personal peace?
And the money, status, and training they get
causes grief from tormentors to cease?
   Why do good people join the Peace Corps?
They can't handle a job nine to five;
they're already victims of past wars;
for a better world they strive.
   Why do good people become missionaries?
They have something good to share;
they want to answer God's call on them,
and truly show they care.

8-10-11

When life hurts and there's noone to blame;
it's just accidents resulting from past wars;
or generational curses from long, long ago,
are you right or wrong to get sore?
   About minor things, every wrong in your life—
just find you some private space,
so those you bombast won't begrudge you,
and the rest of eternity won't be a waste.
   When the whole world is a stage
and surveillance is everywhere,
victims multiply astronomically
and it seems noone gives a care.
   If Jesus had come to the world today,
He could have reached the whole Earth.
Would He be a big hero?
Or would modern-day Pharisees have him cursed?
   Would Jesus be politically correct enough?
Would He have a home where to lay His head?
Would He say all things work to the good?
Would He want or even bother to raise the dead?

                                          8-30-11

Does your past and tradition
have a place in Christianity?
Are they the root
causes of insanity?
  Tho repetitive ruts
can be quite bad,
rejecting your past
might make you quite sad.
  "Make new friends
and keep the old;
one is silver,
and the other's gold."
  This song I learned
as a junior girl scout.
Wise words they are
without a doubt.
  Two lasting gifts
you may give your kids are:
firstly roots, then
wings to fly far.
  These words on a poster
above my mom's bed,
I think about sometimes
tho they don't rule my head.
  I think the past is part
of who you are;
and if you build on it,
you can go far.
  Tho one sure way
to eliminate the past
is for all to forget it
so it doesn't last.
  God, Himself,
changed Jacob's name;
the bible's next chapters
talked of Jacob just the same.

    Adding to your name and past
can, however, be done.
And you can build a future
in the name of Father, Holy Spirit, and Son.

9-10-11

God,
    How to relate to homosexuals
the bible does not teach.
Please enlighten your people,
especially those who preach,
    So that gays may come
to a saving knowledge of You
and make the church more strong
and sexual sins more few.

9-27-11

Peaceably attaining an assets ceiling of one billion dollars:

1) Multibillionaires give up excess assets to persons, organizations, and companies of their choice
2) Promote business education and entrepreneurship.
3) Encourage former multibillionaires to teach and mentor.
4) Research what is the ideal size of each company for their maximum efficiency, and worker and consumer well-being.

10-8-11

Are hospital inmates modern lepers
Whom Pharisees will not touch?
Is Jesus not the cure?
Can love not heal such?
    God helps those who help themselves
within the medical system.
as long as you are able to do so,
there's hope for you, God's children.
    Doctors and aides, divorced from God,
can be scary, to say the least.
You may well feel you are their slaves,
and they treat you like a beast.
    The government wants you to be
a "productive" member of society.
So your aim should truly be
A nine-to-five job, not notoriety.
    Don't forget about your dreams;
Just put them on hold for a while.
They may or may not come about.
Humility makes God smile.
    This might make you feel better:
God prefers hate-love to lukewarm,
in your relations with Him.
Pray that a steadfast heart, he'll form.
    A steadfast heart He likes best;
So don't be wishy-washy either.
Always come back to God
when you get a breather.

10-22-11

How to promote more jobs:
- promote skills existing businesses would hire, (businesses and industries can do).
- promote industries people who need work have the skills to do, (for foreign market if product is not in demand enough here).
- promote industries that produce goods and services existing consumers need, and would buy, (free market does).
- promote environment-friendly products (government can do).
- promote environment-friendly industries, government can do).
- promote worker-friendly industries, (labor unions can do)
- promote consumer-friendly products and services (government can do)
- promote the most efficient size for each business (research grants).

A planned economy must be in God's plan to continue and thrive, and not fail as the USSR's planned economy did.

God's government is a kingdom.

Keep on dreaming of living in a perfect world.

Pray: Thy kingdom come, thy will be done, on Earth as it is in heaven.

Imagine God's kingdom.

10-23-11

Regardless of your relationship with God,
some sins are likely to be judged;
new generations, in growing up,
your reputation could smudge.
  So own your mistakes?
And say the buck stops where?
Are we on the eve of destruction?
who continues la guerre?*
  It is the goodness of God
that brings persons to repentance,
not judgment, says the bible.**
So seek God for your deliverance.
  Blessed is he, the bible says,
who is conscious of his own sin.***
So love your neighbors; do not judge,
and everybody wins.

*the war (French word)
**Romans 2:4
***Matthew 5:3

10-27-11

The Law condemns (even) the best of us;
Grace saves (even) the worst.*
so we're all in need of Jesus
who said the last shall be first.**

Where sin abounds, grace much more abounds.***

  Should we continue in sin
that grace may more abound?
and strive to be the last
for in Jesus to be found?
  The bible says: No,
we must have a change of heart
and walk in the newness of life
so God's kingdom starts.****
  You may lose your sense of reverence
if you live in sin.
Almighty, holy, God
desires that all souls win.*****
  Separation from God
is not desirable for anyone.
God being with you
brings joy, happiness, and fun.

*Joseph Prince, Trinity Broadcasting Network, October 2011
**Matthew 20:16
***Romans 5:20
****Romans 6:1
*****2 Peter 3:9; 1 Thessalonians 5:15

10-31-11

How to attain a spirit of reverence:

- acknowledge God's sovereignty
- admire God's creation around you
- pray
- listen to God's Word preached and taught
- acknowledge God's goodness and justice
- be aware of your own sins
- repent
- develop respectable qualities in yourself
- be salt and light, for God, to other people
- be more humble
- listen to the Holy Spirit
- love; receive love
- give; have a generous heart
- be grateful; express gratitude
- enjoy

10-28-11

MORE PRAYERS

Holy Spirit, thank you
for all You do for me,
guiding me as I write
and helping me to see.
   I praise You for Your persistence
tho sometimes I didn't listen to You,
amidst demons tormenting
when I was feeling blue.
   Anger, confusion, paranoia in me
must have saddened You so.
I love You, the God within,
keeping me from too much woe.

6-7-09

Thank You, God, for sunshine
that keeps me warm all year.
Thank You for good sounds
that give my spirit good cheer.
Thank You, God, for people I enjoy
who make my life worth living.
Thank You for funds sufficient
for occasionally giving.
Thank You, God, for the food I eat
and the exercise I get to do.
Thank You for plenty of rest I have
and for my bible to learn about You.
Thank You, God, for my paper and ink
and for thoughts to express myself.
Thank you for those who read what I write
and for books upon the shelf.
Thank you much for peace and harmony
and for the birds I'm hearing just now.
Thank You for people who work real hard
and for sweat upon the brow.
Thank You, God, for this tasty Chrystal Light
and for all that smells good to me.
Thank You that life is not too harsh
and for all I am able to see.

8-28-10

God, some requests:
Make me reflect You in my life
in all I am, think, say, have, and do.
Make me a more complete human person.
Use me as a means to Your good ends.
Bless me to be a blessing—
a channel of blessings,
making others more for You.
Where I am weak, You are strong in me.
Help me to value my weaknesses where You do,
and to embrace what You like in me.
Show me how to be.
Show me what to do.
Give me words to express
what You would have me think, say, and write.
Show me what to keep, what to throw away.
Make me know Your will for me and
help me know my own will in You.
Guide my choices.
Give me good direction, goals, and purpose.

1-5-11

God please help me
all day long
not to swear
nor do what's wrong.
  Each day fill me
Holy Spirit, I pray.
Help me reflect You
in all I do and say.
  Make me tolerant
of everything I should be.
Make all anger righteous
so I become all I would be.
  Show me good ways
that I should give
to any who need me
so we truly do live.

8-5-11

It's All-Hallows Evening
so I pray for all kids,
that harm does not come
that none do as Satan bids.
   I pray for healthy
amounts of fears;
that later setbacks
won't prevent good careers.
   I pray that each child
learns to discern well,
to keep themselves and others
out of hell.
   I pray all adults
have healthy fear too
and for guidance for the vulnerable
to live lives not too blue.

10-31-11